W9-DDK-100

A LITTLE
Maine
Cookbook

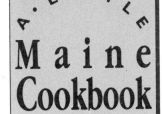

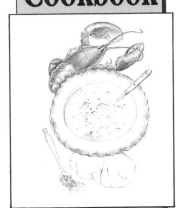

Barbara Karoff

ILLUSTRATED BY
GAIL ROTH

Chronicle Books

First published in 1995 by
The Appletree Press Ltd
19–21 Alfred Street, Belfast BT2 8DL
Tel. +44 232 243074 Fax +44 232 246756
Copyright © 1995 The Appletree Press, Ltd.
Printed in the E.U. All rights reserved.
No part of this publication may be reproduced or
transmitted in any form or by any means, electronic
or mechanical, photocopying, recording or any information
and retrieval system, without permission in writing from
Chronicle Books.

A Little Maine Cookbook

First published in the United States in 1995 by
Chronicle Books, 275 Fifth Street,
San Francisco, CA 94103

ISBN 0-8118-0929-3

9 8 7 6 5 4 3 2 1

A note on measures
Spoon measures are level. All recipes are for
four unless otherwise indicated.

Introduction

The seasons reign supreme in Maine. Winters are long and hard, and summers are short and hot. Summers begin officially on the Fourth of July and the frost is on the pumpkin by September.

To many people, Maine is a state of mind, often associated with lonely outposts and rugged individualists who live in near isolation much of the year. Wherever the people of Maine live, however, whether along the evergreen and island-studded coast, in the far northern woods, or in the busy cities, they eat well.

Blueberries and lobster are the state's most important contribution to our culinary plenty. Almost the entire United States blueberry crop is grown along the Maine coast where the tiny wild berries are eagerly sought after in July and August. The early colonists sun-dried and used them in place of raisins. Today, much of the cultivated crop is frozen and available year round.

Besides its famous lobster, Maine's cold Atlantic waters are well known for clams, oysters, scallops, mussels, and salmon, and the fall hunting season fills many larders with venison and wild game birds.

Down-easters, as Maine residents are called, are fond of desserts. The local Indians made maple syrup before the Europeans arrived and maple products remain important today.

Spring and summer bounty includes rhubarb and fiddlehead ferns, corn and tomatoes. Potatoes are an important crop and pumpkins and cranberries add color and zest to the fall harvest.

Most Maine cooking is not elaborate. It is good solid American fare that respects the seasons and takes advantage of local products.

Finnan Haddie Chowder

Finnan Haddie (smoked fish) has been part of the New England diet since colonial times. This chowder is baked in the oven and may be served at the table directly from the casserole dish.

1 lb thick finnan haddie fillet	1 bay leaf
1/2 cup butter	salt and pepper
2 onions, thinly sliced	4 cups milk, approx.
2 baking potatoes, peeled, diced	minced chives and/or parsley

In a shallow dish, cover fish with cold water and soak for at least 1 hour. In a medium skillet, melt 4 tablespoons butter, add onions and potatoes and cook until onion is golden. Place vegetables, along with remaining butter, in a shallow 1 1/2 quart casserole dish. Break fish into bite-size pieces and place on top along with bay leaf and salt and pepper to taste. Pour enough milk over to completely cover the fish. Cover the casserole dish and bake at 350°F for 45 minutes. Remove bay leaf and ladle into bowls. Top with minced chives and/or parsley.

Lobster Stew

Lobster stew is simple, traditional and always delicious. The lobster meat may be bought already cooked, or you can cook a live lobster by boiling or steaming it, and removing the meat.

½ cup butter	¼ tsp paprika
2 cups cooked lobster meat,	3 cups milk
cut up	2 cups half-and-half cream
½ tsp salt	

Melt butter in a large pot. Add the lobster and sprinkle with salt and paprika. Heat thoroughly. Add milk and half-and-half cream and heat, stirring, just to boiling point. Serve at once in heated bowls.

Corn and Pumpkin Chowder

The hearty flavors of summer and fall are combined in this robust soup.

2 tbsp butter	½ tsp ground cumin
2 medium onions, chopped	generous ¾ cup half-and-half
1 cup corn kernels, fresh or frozen	cream
1 cup cooked pumpkin, fresh	generous ¾ cup milk
or canned	salt
3 cups chicken stock	chopped cilantro or parsley

In a large pan, melt butter and sauté onions until soft. Purée corn in food processor or blender. Add corn, pumpkin, stock, and cumin to onions. Mix well. Simmer 20 minutes. Add half-and-half cream, milk, and salt to taste. Garnish with cilantro or parsley.

Clam Chowder

Clam chowder is, of course, a Maine tradition and is as welcome on a foggy summer evening as on a blizzardy winter night.

---

3 cups clams, with clam juice
1 1/2-inch cube salt pork, finely diced or
3 slices bacon, finely diced
1 onion, finely chopped
3 medium baking potatoes, peeled, diced
3 cups milk or half-and-half cream
2 tbsp butter
salt and pepper

Mince clams and set aside with their juice. In a skillet, sauté salt pork or bacon until crisp. Strain and set bits aside. In a large pot, sauté onions in 2 tablespoons of the rendered fat until golden. Add potatoes and clam juice and simmer 10 minutes, or until potatoes are tender. Add milk, butter, and salt and pepper to taste. Heat until butter melts. Serve with a few pork or bacon bits on top of each serving.

Cold Blueberry Soup

Maine residents are so fond of wild blueberries that they have devised a number of unusual and delicious ways in which to use them. This light and delicate soup, made with freshly picked, wild Maine blueberries, is a fine beginning (or even an ending) to a summer meal, but it is good with cultivated blueberries as well.

---

2 cups water
2 cups blueberries
zest of 1/2 lemon
zest of 1/2 orange
3-inch cinnamon stick
1/4–1/2 cup sugar, to taste
generous 2/3 cup dry red wine
1 cup sour cream or plain yogurt

Combine water, blueberries, lemon zest, orange zest, cinnamon, and sugar in a medium pot. Bring to a boil and simmer, uncovered, for 15 minutes. Add the wine and simmer 5 minutes. Strain into a bowl to chill. When very cold, whisk in sour cream or yogurt. Refrigerate until icy cold and serve.

Maine Potato Salad with Green Beans

When locally grown green beans are paired with locally grown new potatoes, the result is a special treat. It's rather like a Salade Niçoise, but without the tuna and anchovies.

3 lb new potatoes	**Vinaigrette:**
1 1/2 lb green beans	6 tbsp extra-virgin olive oil
24 black olives, preferably	2 tbsp balsamic or
Mediterranean	red wine vinegar
6 tbsp minced parsley	
salt and pepper	
(serves 8–10)	

Peel potatoes (if desired) and boil in a medium pot until tender. Drain well, slice into thick pieces, and dress with *vinaigrette* while still warm. Trim green beans, cut into thirds, and steam until crisp but tender (i.e. not mushy and soft). Dress with *vinaigrette* while still warm. Remove seeds from olives (a cherry pitter works well) and cut into thirds. Combine potatoes, beans, olives, and parsley. Mix gently, but thoroughly. Add more *vinaigrette*, if necessary, and salt and pepper to taste. Serve at room temperature.

Stuffed Beet Salad

This festive salad is very attractive, and much more interesting than the usual cold, pickled beet offering. It may be prepared early in the day and refrigerated until serving time.

8 medium beet, cooked, peeled	1 tbsp minced red bell pepper
2 tbsp cream cheese, softened	mayonnaise
1 tbsp minced celery	lettuce
1 tbsp minced green onion	

With a sharp knife, carefully carve out a cavity in the center of each beet. Mince the extracted beet and combine in a bowl with the cream cheese, celery, onion, and bell pepper. Add just enough mayonnaise to hold the mixture together. Fill the beet cavities with the mixture and chill. Carefully slice the stuffed beet into half-inch slices. Serve on a bed of lettuce.

Spring Fiddleheads

After the long Maine winter, the curled fern fronds called fiddleheads herald spring when they make their brief appearance in May. The season lasts only about two weeks and fiddleheads must be cooked within a few hours of picking.

To prepare fiddleheads, the light brown fuzz must be removed first. Trim the stem ends, place fiddleheads in a large pot of cold water and stir. Change water and repeat until fuzz is gone. Put the fiddleheads in a steamer and steam until just tender, then sauté lightly in butter or olive oil and serve at once.

Fiddleheads are also delicious with pasta. Sauté strips of red bell pepper and a clove of minced garlic in olive oil. When the peppers are almost done, slice and add the steamed fiddleheads and sauté gently for 2–3 minutes. Combine with freshly cooked, drained pasta and a little more olive oil, if needed.

Mashed Potatoes for Garlic Lovers

These potatoes are aromatic and flavorful. They are delicious with just about any kind of meat, poultry, or fish. Use your best extra-virgin olive oil and don't skimp on the garlic!

---

2 large baking potatoes
6 peeled cloves of garlic to taste (use more garlic if desired)
extra-virgin olive oil
salt and pepper

Peel the potatoes and cut them into chunks. Slice the garlic cloves in half. Boil the potatoes and garlic until very tender in lightly salted water. Drain. Mash potatoes and garlic together. Add 2–3 tbsp olive oil (or to taste) and season with salt and pepper.

Fresh Corn Pudding

When the long-awaited local corn is piled high at the roadside farm stands, the people of Maine consume it in large quantities. During the short season, corn comes to the table prepared in many ways. Fresh Corn Pudding is a favorite and more elaborate alternative to "on the cob".

---

6 large ears corn	*¹/₂ cup milk, scalded*
4 eggs, beaten	*1 tbsp minced parsley*
2 tbsp butter	*salt*
2 tbsp sugar	

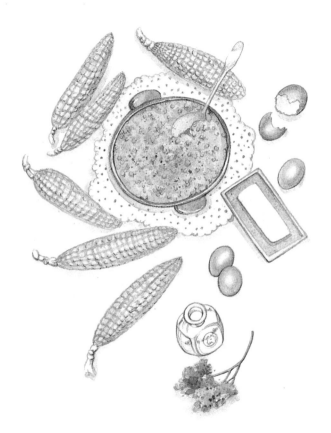

Cut corn kernels off cobs into a shallow bowl. Scrape cobs with a knife to extract liquid and add it, with the beaten eggs, to corn. Place butter in a 1-quart baking dish and heat in oven to melt butter. Dredge dish with melted butter and add excess to corn along with sugar, milk, parsley and salt. Pour mixture into buttered dish and place dish in a pan with hot water half way up the sides of the dish. Bake at 350°F for about 1 hour or until set.

Grilled Corn on the Cob
with Herb Butter

When the barbecue is fired up, this is an excellent way to prepare fresh summer corn. Cilantro, parsley, chives, or dill are all good herb choices for the butter.

To make herb butter: Combine 3 tbsp minced herbs with 8 tbsp soft butter. Chill before using.

Remove the silk from ears of corn but do not remove the husks. Gently pull husks back and spread the kernels with herb butter. Pull the husks back into place. Set the cobs on a rack over a medium-hot charcoal fire. Grill for approximately 10 minutes, turning from time to time. Then pull back husks and continue to grill for 2–3 minutes, to brown lightly. Serve with additional herb butter.

Winter Squash with Maine Syrup and Cranberries

This tasty vegetable dish is especially appropriate to prepare when the rest of the meal is also being baked in the oven. Everything can go in together. The squash are especially compatible with roast chicken or turkey.

---

2 sweet dumpling or small acorn squash
2/3 cup dried cranberries
4 tbsp butter
8 tbsp maple syrup

Wash the squash and cut each in half horizontally. Remove seeds. Puncture squash with a fork in several places. Place on a baking sheet, cover sheet tightly with foil and bake at 350°F for 30 minutes. Soak the cranberries in hot water to cover for 5 minutes. Drain well. In a small saucepan, heat the butter and syrup until butter melts. Stir in the cranberries. Divide the mixture among the four squash halves and continue to bake, uncovered, for 10 minutes or until the squash is tender. Serve as a vegetable, one half squash per serving.

Brandied Pumpkin Soufflé

This is a festive fall and winter dish that never fails to win compliments for the cook. It is similar to a soufflé and easy to prepare, but it must be served as soon as it emerges from the oven. It's perfect for Thanksgiving and can go in to bake after the turkey has come from the oven.

---

2 cups cooked pumpkin, fresh or canned
1/2 cup hot milk
1/4 cup brandy
6 tbsp sugar
4 tbsp butter, melted
1/4 tsp cayenne pepper
1/4 tsp grated nutmeg
1/4 tsp salt
1 tsp finely grated lemon peel
4 egg yolks, well beaten
4 egg whites

In a large bowl combine pumpkin, milk, brandy, sugar and butter and mix until smooth. Add cayenne pepper, nutmeg, salt, lemon peel, and egg yolks. Beat egg whites to medium stiff peaks and fold in. Turn the mixture into a buttered 1-quart soufflé dish. Bake at 400°F for 25–30 minutes or until well puffed and slightly browned. Serve immediately.

Maine Lobster Bake
with all the Trimmings

Maine's long, rugged, sea coast and many off-shore islands have been the setting for lobster and clam bakes for as long as lobsters have been pulled from the sea and clams have been dug from the beaches. It's possible to stage a lobster bake in your back garden, but the seaweed and the seawater that impart so much authentic flavor will be missing and, anyway, it's more fun to cook and eat by the sea.

This is how "down-easters" stage a lobster bake on a beach in Maine without the mess of digging a pit and getting sand in the food. How much food to prepare depends on the number of people to be fed but, because the complete meal includes a substantial amount of food, the following quantities are probably enough for one person. Multiply by the number of people to be fed and secure a clean galvanized wash tub of appropriate size.

The first priority is to choose a beautiful location by the sea. Gather enough large rocks to support the wash tub about a foot off the beach so that a fire can be kept going beneath it.

Have ready for each person: one lobster, ($1\frac{1}{4}$lb is a good size) six to twelve steamer clams and the same number of mussels, and one or two ears of corn. The lobsters must be live, the clams and mussels tightly closed, and part of the husks must remain on the corn.

Send someone out to gather fresh seaweed. Place about 2 inches of salt water in the tub. Build a good hot fire under the tub and bring the water to a rapid boil. Add the live lobsters and cover them with a layer of seaweed. Add the clams and mussels and cover them with a thin layer of seaweed. Then add the ears of corn.

Cover again with seaweed and stoke the fire which should be roaring hot.

In about 20 minutes, check the contents of the tub. The lobsters are done when they turn red. The clams and mussels are done when they open. (Discard any that do not.) The corn is done when it is tender. In the meantime, melt about $^3/_4$ cup of butter per person. When the food is ready to be served, give each person a large plate, a lobster, clams, mussels, corn and a cup of melted butter for dipping. Don't forget the lobster crackers and picks.

Settle back, dig in, and enjoy a quintessential Maine feast.

Grilled Salmon en Brochette

Salmon never tasted better than it does with this simple marinade.

---

3 tbsp olive oil
2 tbsp lemon juice
$^1/_2$ tsp salt
freshly ground pepper
2 tbsp chopped fresh dill
1$^1/_2$ lb salmon steaks, cut into $^1/_2$-inch cubes
$^2/_3$ lb mushroom caps

In a shallow dish, combine olive oil, lemon juice, salt, pepper, and dill. Add the salmon and marinate for 30 minutes. Thread the salmon on metal skewers alternately with the mushrooms. Brush with marinade and grill over hot coals for 6 minutes, rotating skewers several times. Brush with marinade while cooking.

Old Time Maine Seafood Casserole

The distinctive flavors of shrimp, crab, and scallops combine beautifully in this popular dish.

$^1/_2$ lb shrimp, shelled
$^1/_2$ lb crab meat, picked over
$^3/_4$ lb scallops (if large, cut in half)
$^1/_2$ cup butter
I small onion, finely chopped
$^1/_2$ green or red bell pepper, finely chopped
$^1/_4$ cup flour
I $^1/_2$ cup milk
2 tbsp sherry
I cup soft bread crumbs

Combine shrimp, crab, and scallops in a bowl and set aside. In a large skillet, sauté onion and bell pepper in butter until soft. Add flour and mix well. Slowly stir in milk and cook until slightly thickened. Stir in sherry and combine with seafood.

Spoon into a buttered shallow dish or into individual *au gratin* dishes. Sprinkle with bread crumbs, and bake at 400°F for 15 minutes.

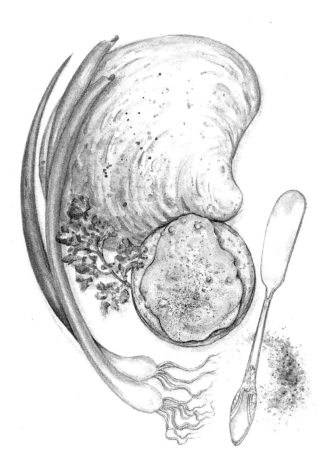

Savory Clam Bites

The clam mixture can be made ahead for this quick and easy appetizer.

---

4 oz cream cheese	salt
2 tbsp heavy cream	2 green onions, minced
7 oz minced clams, drained	paprika
pinch of dry mustard	toasted baguette slices or
few drops of Tabasco	melba rounds
2 tbsp minced parsley	

(makes 24)

In a large bowl, combine all ingredients except paprika and baguette slices. Spread the clam mixture on toasted baguette slices and place them on baking sheet. Broil a few inches from the heat until tops are puffed, 2–3 minutes. Sprinkle with paprika and serve hot.

Scalloped Oysters

According to one source, scalloped oysters are so named because they were originally baked in scallop shells.

---

3 cups cream cracker crumbs or	1/3 cup minced parsley
dry bread crumbs	1 tbsp fresh thyme or 1/2 tsp dried
6 cups shucked oysters	1/4 tsp grated nutmeg
12 tbsp butter	salt and pepper
1/3 cup finely chopped green onion	

Spread half the crumbs in a buttered shallow baking dish. Drain the oysters and arrange them on top of the crumbs in a single layer. In a small skillet, melt the butter and sauté the onions for 2 minutes. Add the remaining ingredients to the butter and pour half over the oysters. Cover with remaining crumbs and then with the remaining butter. Bake at 450°F for 7–10 minutes, until brown and crisp.

Baked Wild Duck Breasts

Much of Maine is wooded and in the fall hunters from all over New England take to the Maine woods. Moose, deer and bear, beaver, and rabbit all attract the sportsmen as do pheasant, woodcock, geese, and a variety of ducks. Baked duck breasts are an elegant change from the whole roasted bird. This dish must be started a day in advance.

---

4 duck breasts, cut in half	8 slices bacon
salt and pepper	1 cup dry white wine
juice of 1 lemon	

Remove skin from duck breasts. Soak the meat overnight in water to which 2 tablespoons salt and 1 tablespoon baking soda have been added. After soaking breasts, rinse with fresh water and pat dry. Arrange breasts in a single layer in a shallow roasting pan. Sprinkle with salt, pepper, and lemon juice. Top each piece of meat with a slice of bacon. Bake at 375°F for 40 minutes basting with white wine and pan juices.

Remove breasts to serving platter. Deglaze the pan with remaining wine and reduce slightly. Serve the sauce with the meat.

Roast Venison

Venison sometimes has an overly strong flavor and can be less tender than desired. Marinating it overnight in a flavorful mixture of wine, onions, tomato sauce, and herbs works wonders, not only improving the flavor, but tenderizing the meat as well. Start this recipe a day in advance of serving.

---

venison roast
4 cups dry red wine
1 cup tomato sauce
2 onions, thinly sliced
oregano
$1/2$ lb bacon
$1/2$ lb mushrooms, thinly sliced

Remove all fat from the meat. In a large glass or stainless steel bowl, combine wine, tomato sauce, and onions and marinate the roast in this mixture over night. Turn once or twice. Remove meat and reserve marinade. Preheat oven to 500°F. Dust meat with oregano and cover with slices of bacon. Place in roasting pan in oven, and immediately lower temperature to 350°F. Roast for 30 minutes per pound, basting frequently with reserved marinade. When done and nicely browned, remove meat to a platter. Add mushrooms and remaining marinade to pan juices and reduce over high heat until slightly thickened. Serve this sauce over or with the roast.

Hunter's Venison Casserole

For as long as anyone can remember, venison has been eagerly looked forward to as a fall treat in Maine. In this flavorful casserole, the meat must marinate for 24 hours before being cooked. The sophisticated results are well worth the planning ahead.

---

2 1/2 lb boneless venison, cubed	3 whole cloves
flour for dredging	1 tsp dried thyme
vegetable oil for browning	1 cup celery leaves, chopped
chicken stock	4 sprigs parsley, chopped
1 tbsp butter	**Bouquet Garni:**
1/2 lb mushrooms	3 sprigs parsley
2 oz red currant jelly	1 clove garlic, cut in half
Marinade:	2 green onions, chopped
2 cups dry red wine	7 shallots, chopped
10 peppercorns	1 stalk celery, chopped
2 bay leaves	

In a bowl large enough to hold the roast, combine marinade ingredients, add venison, and refrigerate, covered, for 24 hours. Strain off marinade and reserve. Pat meat dry and dredge with flour. In a large skillet, brown lightly in oil. Transfer to a large, heavy pot and pour over half of the marinade and half of the chicken stock or just enough to cover. Tie the *bouquet garni* ingredients together in a cheesecloth bag and add to the pot. Simmer for 1 hour. Remove *bouquet garni* and continue simmering for 2 hours, adding more liquid as necessary. In a skillet, sauté the mushrooms in butter. Add jelly and, when jelly is melted, stir into venison. Adjust seasoning and serve.

Maple Sugar-Glazed Ham

This sweet and spicy glaze adds the perfect finish to any baked ham, but is especially good on the home-cured country variety.

---

³/₄ cup maple syrup
¹/₄ cup cider vinegar
1 tsp dry mustard
pinch of ground cloves

In a small pan, combine all ingredients and boil gently until slightly thickened. Baste ham liberally with glaze as it bakes.

Banana-Blueberry Oatmeal Bread

Bananas make this not-too-sweet quick bread very moist. Be sure to bake it until it is no longer sticky in the center when tested with a skewer. It slices best if wrapped in foil after cooling and refrigerated for several hours.

---

1 cup whole wheat flour
1/2 cup all-purpose flour
2/3 cup sugar
2 tsp baking powder
1/4 tsp salt
3/4 cup quick cooking rolled oats
1/3 cup vegetable oil
2 eggs, lightly beaten
2 bananas, mashed
1 cup blueberries

In a large bowl, combine flours, sugar, baking powder, salt, and oats. In a separate bowl, combine oil, eggs, and bananas and add to dry ingredients.

Stir in blueberries. Spoon into buttered 9 x 5 x 3-inch loaf pan and bake at 350°F for one hour or until the loaf is no longer sticky in the center when tested with a wooden skewer. Cool 10 minutes in pan and remove to rack to cool completely.

Blueberry Muffins

Summer in Maine is blueberry time, and groups and individuals take regularly to the woods and shores seeking the tiny, bursting with flavor, wild berries which State-of-Mainers prefer. The larger, cultivated variety, available fresh in season and frozen year round, are sold in most supermarkets, and are good, too.

2½ cups all-purpose flour	1 egg
4 tsp baking powder	1 cup milk
¼ cup sugar	4 tbsp melted shortening
½ tsp salt	1 cup blueberries
1 tbsp grated orange peel	
(makes 24)	

Combine dry ingredients and orange peel in a large bowl. In a separate bowl, beat egg, combine with milk and melted shortening, and add to the dry ingredients. Fold in blueberries. Batter will be very stiff. Spoon into small greased muffin pans and bake at 425°F until muffins test done.

Maple Muffins

Maple muffins are a simple and easily prepared treat that turn an ordinary breakfast into a special occasion. The elusive maple flavor has a natural affinity for ham or sausage and, because the muffins are slightly sweet, they require no jam or honey.

1/4 cup milk	1/4 tsp salt
1 egg	3/4 cup maple syrup
1 3/4 cup all-purpose flour	1/4 cup butter, melted
2 1/2 tsp baking powder	2/3 cup chopped pecans

(makes 10)

In a small bowl, beat milk and egg together. Combine dry ingredients in a large bowl. Add egg and milk mixture alternately with maple syrup. Fold in melted butter and pecans. Spoon into greased muffin pans and bake at 325°F until a wooden skewer inserted in the center of a muffin comes out clean.

Strawberry-Rhubarb Pie

Rhubarb – often called pie plant – and strawberries are among the first harbingers of spring. They are a delicious combination in this pie. Prepare your favorite pastry for a 9-inch double crust pie and line a 9-inch pie plate with bottom crust. Roll pastry for top crust and set aside.

3 tbsp cornstarch
1 cup sugar
pinch of salt
4 cups sliced rhubarb, cut in 1/2-in pieces
1 basket / 2 cups strawberries, hulled, cut in half if large
1 tsp grated orange peel
2 tbsp butter

Combine cornstarch, sugar, and salt in a large bowl. Add the rhubarb, strawberries, and orange peel. Toss well and spoon into prepared crust. Dot with butter and cover with top crust. Cut several vents in top. Bake at 425°F for 20 minutes. Reduce heat to 350°F and bake until crust is nicely browned, about 30 minutes. Cool on a rack. This pie is delicious on its own but may also be served with vanilla ice cream.

Winter Snow Iced Cream

An old Maine treat – when the weather cooperates!

---

sugar
2 cups heavy cream
1 tsp vanilla extract
newly fallen clean snow

In a large bowl, add sugar to cream until it is quite sweet and stir to dissolve. Add vanilla. Refrigerate until very cold. Just before serving, beat clean, newly fallen snow into the cream until the mixture is very stiff. Serve immediately.

Blueberry Gingerbread

The old-fashioned taste of gingerbread combines well with blueberries in this time-tested Maine favorite.

½ cup butter	*1 tsp ground ginger*
½ cup brown sugar, firmly packed	*1 tsp ground cinnamon*
1 cup molasses	*½ tsp ground cloves*
1 egg	*½ tsp salt*
2½ cups all-purpose flour	*1 cup hot water*
1 tsp baking powder	*1¼ cup blueberries*

In a medium bowl, cream butter and sugar. Add molasses and beat until light. Add egg and beat well. In a separate bowl, combine dry ingredients and add 1 tablespoon to the blueberries. (Do not do this if using frozen berries or they will become sticky.) Add dry ingredients to the creamed mixture alternately with hot water. Beat until smooth and fold in the blueberries. Bake in buttered 8-inch square pan at 350°F for 35 minutes, or until a wooden skewer inserted in the center comes out clean.

Maple Sour Cream Cup Cakes

These simple, fine-textured cup cakes are very easy to prepare. If maple sugar is unavailable, substitute brown sugar.

---

1 egg
sour cream, approximately 1 cup

1 cup maple sugar
1 tsp cream of tartare
1 tsp baking soda
1 1/2 cups all-purpose flour
(makes 12)

Break the egg into a 1-cup measure. Fill measure with sour cream and spoon into a mixing bowl. Add remaining ingredients and beat well to combine. Spoon into greased muffin pans and bake at 375°F until a wooden skewer inserted in the center comes out clean. Frost with icing or dust with powdered sugar, if desired.

Indian Pudding

Indian Pudding, of which there are many versions, is a favorite throughout New England. It's best served warm with vanilla ice cream.

---

4 cups milk	2/3 cup molasses
1 cup yellow cornmeal	3/4 tsp salt
2 eggs, beaten	1/4 tsp ground cinnamon
1/2 cup brown sugar	1/4 tsp ground ginger

In a medium saucepan, heat milk, but do not boil. Stir in cornmeal and continue to stir until thickened. Remove from heat and allow to cool slightly, add eggs, and mix well. Add remaining ingredients. Pour into a buttered 1-quart baking dish and bake at 325°F for 2 hours.

Cranberry-Maple Drop Cookies

These are old-fashioned cookies that are perfect with a glass of milk or a cup of tea.

---

³/₄ cup dried cranberries	*2¹/₂ cups all-purpose flour*
¹/₂ cup sour cream	*¹/₂ tsp ground cinnamon*
¹/₂ tsp baking soda	*¹/₂ tsp ground cloves*
¹/₂ cup maple or brown sugar	*¹/₂ tsp ground nutmeg*
¹/₂ cup molasses	*pinch of salt*
1 egg	*²/₃ cup chopped walnuts, optional*
(makes approx. 50 cookies)	

Place cranberries in a small bowl and cover with hot water. In a large bowl, whisk together sour cream, baking soda, sugar, molasses, and egg until well blended. In a separate bowl, combine dry ingredients and stir into sour cream mixture. Drain cranberries and fold in along with nuts, if using. Drop by spoonfuls on greased baking tray. They do not spread. Bake at 375°F for 12–15 minutes. Cool on rack and store air tight.

Egg Coffee

In this recipe, an old Maine secret is revealed. Prepared this way, coffee can be reheated with good results and it can stand for up to 12 hours without becoming stale. It's a useful trick to know about when planning ahead for a large gathering.

4 cups fresh cold water
I egg
5 tbsp freshly ground coffee

Heat the water in a stainless steel or glass coffee pot. Break the egg, shell and all, into a bowl. Stir in the ground coffee and a little water. When the water in the pot boils, add the coffee and egg mixture and stir until the coffee boils less rapidly. Adjust the heat and boil for 5 minutes. Let stand 5 minutes then serve.

Raspberry Shrub

This simple drink is wonderfully refreshing – perfect for a sultry summer afternoon. Shrubs are of colonial origin, and they were spiked with brandy or rum. Today's non-alcoholic versions are served over ice or water.

5 qts fresh raspberries
approx. 2 qts cider vinegar
sugar

Wash berries and place them in a glass or stainless steel pot. Add vinegar to just cover the berries and let stand for 24 hours. Press the mixture through a sieve lined with cheesecloth. For each cup of liquid, add I cup of sugar. Boil gently for 20 minutes. Cool and pour into clean jars or bottles. Store in a cool place. To serve: Place 2–3 spoonfuls of the syrup in a tall glass and fill it with cold water or crushed ice.

Bread-and-Butter Pickles

Always popular, bread-and-butter pickles are perfect with sandwiches.

---

8 cups thinly sliced cucumbers, unpeeled
2 large onions, thinly sliced
salt
2 cups cider vinegar
2 tsp celery seed
3 cups sugar
2 tsp turmeric
3-inch stick cinnamon
2 green peppers, seeded, finely chopped
2 red peppers, seeded, finely chopped
(makes 4 pints)

Combine cucumbers and onions in a stainless steel pot. Sprinkle generously with salt. Set aside for at least 1 hour. Drain accumulated liquid, add remaining ingredients and bring to a boil. Boil gently for 30–45 minutes. Stir frequently. Pack in sterilized jars and seal while hot.

Watermelon Pickles

Maine cooks make this old favorite in the summer when watermelons are at their peak.

To prepare rind: Select melons with a thick, tender rind. Cut off dark green skin and remove pink pulp. Cut rind into 1-inch squares and weigh them. You will need 3 lb. Place rind in a large pot, cover with salted water ($^1/_4$ cup salt to 4 cups water) and simmer 30 minutes. Drain. Cover with fresh water. Simmer 10 minutes. Drain. Cover with fresh water. Simmer 10 minutes and let stand over night. Drain.

For Syrup:
6 cups cider vinegar
1 $^1/_2$ cups water
3 lb sugar
2 tbsp whole cloves
1 cinnamon stick, broken up
(makes 3–4 pints)

Combine syrup ingredients in a large pot and simmer until the sugar dissolves. Add the prepared rind and simmer gently until rind is clear and syrup is thick, about 1 hour. Pack into sterilized jars and seal.

Index